Excellence in Teaching with the Seven Laws

- **EXPLAINS** how and why excellent teachers practice their profession.

- **USEFUL** for teaching in schools, the university, in business, and other situations—for the educational development of youth and adults.

- **WRITTEN** with freighted, yet simple words, sentences, and paragraphs—with practical ideas for effective teaching and student learning.

- **DISTILLS** the art of masterful teaching into seven easy-to-understand laws and principles.

- **DEVELOPS** each law with practical guidelines—preparing for and the process of artful teaching.

- **BASED** on sound psychological and educational principles of how learning is transmitted from one mind to another and into actions.

- **PRESENTS** fresh insights for both new and experienced teachers, in order to be excellent in their teaching.

- **IDEAL** for those, without formal education training, who are called upon to teach or train in the university, churches, or business.

- **EXCELLENT** tool for self-study in how-to-teach, as well as a helpful trainer's step-by-step instruction program of teaching methods.

- **INSPIRES** warmhearted and enthusiastic teaching, and the joy of learning in students.

Excellence in Teaching with the Seven Laws

A Contemporary Abridgment of
Gregory's *Seven Laws of Teaching*

Carl Shafer, Ed.D., Editor

BAKER BOOK HOUSE
Grand Rapids, Michigan 49506

ISBN: 0-8010-8261-7

Third printing, November 1986

Printed in the United States of America

As Superintendent of Public Instruction for Michigan, I commend you on the excellent work you have done to update and summarize *The Seven Laws of Teaching* by John Milton Gregory. (Superintendent of Public Instruction, 1859-1865)

With the current focus on improving and strengthening education, the quality of teaching that goes on in the classroom is more important than ever. Gregory's laws are as relevant and basic to excellence in education today as the many more recent research studies on how students learn and how best to teach them.

The teacher is the key to a good education. *Excellence in Teaching with the Seven Laws* emphasizes simple, common sense, and effective ways for students to learn. Although excellent teachers already practice these principles, other teachers could improve their skills by following them.

Thank you for making *The Seven Laws of Teaching* more accessible to today's educators.

Phillip E. Runkel
Superintendent of Public Instruction
State of Michigan

Wanted: good teachers

This paradox underscores an indisputable
fact: good teachers are the absolute
prerequisite for good schools.
Without able and willing teachers,
all reform proposals will come to naught.

Fred M. Hechinger in
Harvard Business Review
January-February 1985, p. 138

Contents

- Expert teachers arouse and direct self-activities by their students, thus stimulating them to learn for themselves.

- Student skills grow with practical exercises involving their minds.

- Excellent education helps learners to be investigative discoverers.

- Real and valuable learning is more than memorization.

- Review perfects knowledge, confirms knowledge, and makes knowledge ready and useful.

- Practical reviews are characteristic of excellent teachers.

- Taken together, the seven laws of teaching are freighted with meaning and will, when fully implemented, produce excellent teaching.

Preface

*E*xcellence in Teaching with the Seven Laws is a summary and updating of *The Seven Laws of Teaching*, a classic volume on education. The laws it presents are classic in their meaning and potential use. They are useful for anyone wishing to be a master teacher, an effective trainer in business, or a successful parent. Few educators are so knowledgeable and skillful as to practice all of these laws to their fullest.

John Milton Gregory formulated and elaborated his *Seven Laws* in 1884. In 1917, Dr. Gregory's original work was revised by William C. Bagley and Warren K. Layton, both of the School of Education, University of Illinois. Dr. Gregory's book, with later revisions, was republished in 1954 and is now in its 23rd printing. The frequent reprintings point to its timelessness and wisdom.

A Baptist minister, Dr. Gregory also distinguished himself in various educational positions: head of the Classical School in Detroit; state superintendent of public instruction in Michigan; president of Kalamazoo College; and president of the University of Illinois.

Appreciation is given to Baker Book House for permission to use Dr. Gregory's writing in this condensed manner.

Editor's Introduction

My first acquaintance with *The Seven Laws of Teaching* was about a year ago. Charles R. Swindoll, the pastor of a large church in California, was speaking on the radio. He referred to *The Seven Laws of Teaching* as a book of great benefit to him as a Bible teacher. He mentioned that the book is difficult to find, but worth the search. I obtained a copy from the publisher. Reading the book convinced me that it would be a rewarding experience for anyone seriously interested in education.

In the dozen or so education classes I have taken, in undergraduate and graduate school, as well as numerous seminars for industrial trainers and Christian educators, *The Seven Laws of Teaching* has never been mentioned or recommended. It is evident, however, that some of its content has found its way over the years into educational theory and practice.

Reading the book, with its 100-year-old style, is like finding the "original scrolls" holding the secrets of effective education. What I have learned from formal education classes and practical experience—which also works as effective education—is included in the seven laws. Yet there is much more to learn from these laws.

Years ago I taught in public schools, and over the years I have taught Sunday school. As a parent, I teach also. I've conducted management-training sessions and more recently have taught, on a part-time basis, university-level classes in business administration. The seven laws have wide application to all these and many more educational situations.

Effective learning is fostered by masterful teaching and by following the guidelines of the seven laws. Even though these laws have been available for a hundred years, each new wave of teachers, trainers, and parents must discover and learn anew for themselves the art of education.

It has been observed by many students on all educational levels that "educators make simple things complex—but teachers make complex things simple!" What student, with a sincere desire to learn, has not been forced, for required credits, to sit and listen to a teacher or professor who drones on and on about a subject hardly intelligible? The exams are a regurgitation of memorized, incomprehensible material. And often discouraged, the student thinks, "This is education?"

Gregory's seven laws of teaching are clear and simple statements of the important factors governing the art of teaching. They are admonitions to practice clear and simple teaching. It is my purpose here to make his language more readable and understandable. My hope is to encourage even greater use of Dr. Gregory's ideas, without losing his wisdom.

Serious students who wish to be masterful teachers will probably be able to think of no more than five or ten masterful teachers in their total educational experience. These artful teachers probably practiced many of the principles outlined in the seven laws. These laws will explain why they were masterful teachers—and how we can become like them. A world of inspiration and joy in learning awaits the students of those of us who will study well—and practice—the seven laws of teaching.

Carl Shafer, Ed.D.
Midland, Michigan

An Introduction to the Seven Laws of Teaching

The seven laws of teaching are not difficult to understand. They are so simple and natural that they almost suggest themselves:

1. The teacher must know the lesson, truth, or art to be taught.
2. The learner must show interest in the lesson.
3. The language used as a medium between teacher and learner must be common to both.
4. The lesson to be mastered must be given in terms of truth already known

by the learner—the unknown must be explained by means of the known.

5. Teaching must arouse the pupils to learn things for themselves.

6. Learning is thinking into one's own understanding a new idea or truth, or working into habit a new art or skill.

7. Teaching must be completed, confirmed, and tested by review, rethinking, and application.

These fundamental laws will be more clearly seen if we state them as rules for teaching:

1. Know thoroughly and be very familiar with the lesson you wish to teach—teach from a full mind and clear understanding.

2. Gain and keep the attention and interest of your pupils. Do not try to teach without their attention.

3. Use words which you and your pupils will understand in the same way. Use clear and vivid language.
4. Begin with what is already well known to the pupil or has been experienced—and proceed to the new material by single, easy, and natural steps—letting the known explain the unknown.
5. Stimulate the pupils' minds to action. Encourage the pupils to think of themselves as discoverers.
6. Require your pupils to reproduce the lesson in thought and action, to work it out in its various phases and applications until it is expressed in the pupils' own language and action.
7. *Review, review, review,* reproducing the old, introducing new thoughts to deepen the impression it has made, adding fresh meaning, finding new applications, correcting any false ideas and completing the true.

Essentials of Successful Teaching

The seven rules, and the laws upon which they are based, underlie and govern all successful teaching. No one who thoroughly masters and uses them need fail as a teacher, if he or she also has the qualities necessary to maintain order. Disorder, noise, and confusion may hinder and prevent the results desired. But good teaching, in itself, will often bring about good order in the classroom.

Like the great laws of nature, these laws of teaching seem clear and obvious. But like other fundamental truths, the simplicity is more apparent than real. The seven laws apply to the teaching of all subjects in all grades, since they are the fundamental conditions under which ideas pass from one mind to another. They are as valid and useful for the instructor in the university as for the teacher in the elementary school. Parents can apply them in dealing with their children, as can managers and supervisors in dealing with their subordinates.

There may be many successful and indeed excellent teachers who have never heard of these laws, and who do not consciously follow them, just as there are many people who walk safely without any theoretical knowledge of gravitation, and talk intelligibly without studying grammar. Like the musician who plays by ear, these natural teachers have learned from practice the laws of teaching, and obey them from habit.

Skill and Enthusiasm

Some might fear that a study of the laws of teaching will tend to result in a cold and mechanical approach rather than warm-hearted and enthusiastic teaching. Not so, because true skill in teaching kindles and keeps alive enthusiasm. Love for teaching grows with the ability to do it well. And enthusiasm will accomplish all the more when guided by intelligence and armed with skill.

Unreflecting superintendents and school boards often prefer enthusiastic teachers to those who are simply well educated or experienced. They believe, and not without reason, that an enthusiastic teacher with lesser learning and skill will accomplish more than will the best-trained and most erudite teacher wholly lacking in zeal. But why choose either the ignorant enthusiast or the educated bore? There is an enthusiasm born of skill, and there is a joy in doing what one can do well. The world's best work, in the schools as in the shops, is done by the calm, steady, and persistent efforts of skilled workmen who know how to keep their tools sharp and utilize every available means to reach their goals.

Sometimes objection to the type of systematic teaching which follows from observing the seven laws has come from pastors, Sunday-school teachers, and others who have assumed that the principal aim of the Sunday school is to impress rather than to instruct. But what exhortation will have permanent power without being supported by some clear truth? If the choice must be between the warmhearted teacher who makes gushing appeals, and the coldhearted one who stifles all feeling by indifference, the former is perhaps to be preferred. But why either? The teacher whose own mind glows with the truth, and who skillfully leads his or her pupils to a clear understanding of the same truth, will have inspirational power too.

As we discuss the seven laws, there will necessarily be some repetitions. The laws are like seven hilltops of different height scattered over the landscape. As we climb each hill, the various points in the landscape will be seen from different views and with a fresh perspective. For the careful student, new applications of the laws will then come to light.

A Word to Teachers in Christian-Education Programs

While facing your pupils, how often have you wished for the power to look into their minds, and to plant there a belief in the gospel? No key will ever open to you the doors of their minds better than will an understanding and practice of the seven laws.

(Note: In order to give the laws their broadest possible application, the word *student, trainee, subordinate,* or *child* may be substituted wherever the term *pupil* appears.)

The Law of the Teacher

The Law

The teacher must know what he or she teaches.

*The teacher must
know what he
or she teaches.*

The Philosophy of the Law

The law that we cannot teach without knowledge seems too simple for proof. How can something come out of nothing, or how can darkness give light? Although this law is virtually a truism, it is also the fundamental essential of teaching. If the law is reversed, another important truth is revealed: *What the teacher knows he or she will teach.*

The word *know* is central in the law of the teacher. Knowledge is the material with which the teacher works. Consider the nature of knowledge. What men call knowledge is of many degrees, from the first glimpse of truth to full understanding. As we gradually acquire knowledge, it will be characterized by (1) faint recognition; (2) the ability to recall for ourselves, or to describe in a general way to others, what we have learned; (3) the power to explain, prove, illustrate, and apply it; and (4) an appreciation of its deeper meaning and an ability to act upon it. That is, our actions will be modified by it. It is this last form of knowledge, or experience, which is important in the law of the true teacher.

It is difficult to teach effectively without fullness of knowledge. At the same time not every one who knows the subject matter thoroughly will necessarily teach successfully. But imperfect knowing will be reflected in imperfect teaching. What teachers do not know they cannot teach successfully. Even if they rigorously follow the other six laws, their teaching will be uncertain and crippled when characterized by an inadequate knowledge of the material to be taught.

A teacher's ready and evident knowledge helps to give the pupils needed confidence. We follow with expectation and delight the guide who has a thorough knowledge of the

---

Law I

The teacher must
know what he
or she teaches.

---

field we wish to explore. But we follow reluctantly and without interest the ignorant and incompetent leader. Children as well as adults object to being taught by one in whom they have no confidence. In some unfortunate cases, great knowledge is unaccompanied by the ability to inspire pupils with a love of study. This is a condition fatal to successful teaching, especially with young pupils. Better a teacher with limited knowledge but with the power to stimulate students.

The first great law of teaching clearly stresses a splendid ideal which no one except Jesus, the Great Teacher, ever fully realized. It is this ideal which every true teacher should try to approach. From the mother teaching her little child, to the instructor of the most abstract science, the orator addressing senates, and the preacher teaching great congregations, this law knows few exceptions and permits few violations.

It is affirmed everywhere: *Teachers must know what they teach.*

Rules for Teachers

1. Prepare each lesson by fresh study. Last year's knowledge has necessarily faded somewhat. Only fresh conceptions inspire us to our best efforts.

2. When teaching new material, find analogies to more familiar facts and principles. Illustrations are an invaluable method in teaching others.

3. Study the lesson until it takes shape in familiar language. The final product of clear thought is clear speech.

4. Find the natural order of the several steps of the lesson. In every subject there is a natural path from the simplest to the most complex ideas.

5. Find the relationship of the lesson to

The teacher must know what he or she teaches.

the lives of the learners. Pupils learn material more readily if the teacher is aware of its practical value.

6. Use freely all legitimate study aids, but never rest until a full understanding is clearly before you.

7. Bear in mind that complete mastery of a few things is better than an ineffective smattering of many things.

8. Have a definite time for study of each lesson well in advance of the teaching. One will keep on learning the lesson which is studied in advance. There will also be opportunity to gather fresh interest and illustrations before teaching.

9. Have a plan of study, but do not hesitate, when necessary, to study beyond the plan. The best approach is to ask and answer these questions about each lesson: What? How? Why?

10. Obtain good books on the subject of your lessons. Buy, borrow, or beg if neces-

sary, but obtain somehow the help of the best thinkers to stimulate your own thought. But do not read without thinking. If possible, talk the lesson over with an intelligent friend. If such aids are unavailable, put your views and thoughts in writing. This may clear up obscurities.

Violations and Mistakes

Our discussion would be incomplete without some mention of the frequent violations of the law of the teacher. The best teachers may spoil their most careful and earnest work by thoughtless blunders. The most effective teachers make as few errors as possible and learn from those which they do make.

1. The very ignorance of pupils may tempt the teacher to neglect careful prepa-

---

Law I

---

*The teacher must
know what he
or she teaches.*

---

ration and study. A teacher may think that in any event he or she will know much more of the lesson than will the pupils. Such teachers imagine that they will find something to say about the lesson, or that their ignorance will pass unnoticed. This is a sad mistake, and one that often costs dearly. The teacher who cheats on preparation is almost sure to be discovered, and from that time the teacher's standing with the class is reduced.

2. Some teachers assume that it is the pupils' work, not theirs, to study the lesson, and that with book in hand, the instructor will easily be able to ascertain whether the pupils have learned. It would be better to let one of the pupils who knows the lesson examine the others, than for the teacher to discourage study by revealing his or her own indifference and lack of preparation.

3. Some teachers look hastily through the lesson, and conclude that though they have

not thoroughly mastered it, or perhaps any part of it, they have gathered enough to fill the period, and can, if necessary, supplement the little they know with random talk and stories. Or, lacking time or heart for any preparation, they dismiss all thought of teaching, and fill the hour with ill-chosen exercises, hoping that the pupils will receive some benefit from mere attendance.

4. A more serious mistake is that of those teachers who, failing to find stimulation in the lesson, make it a mere framework upon which to hang some fancies of their own.

5. An even larger wrong is committed by teachers who seek to conceal their lazy ignorance with some pompous pretense of learning. These ineffectives hide their lack of knowledge by an array of high-sounding phrases beyond the comprehension of their students. They utter solemn platitudes in a wise tone, or pretend to possess profound information. Who has not seen such shams

*The teacher must
know what he
or she teaches.*

practiced upon pupils in the name of education?

Thus, many teachers try to practice their profession either partly prepared or wholly unprepared. They are like messengers without a message. They lack entirely the power and enthusiasm necessary to produce the fruits which we have a right to look for from their efforts. Obey this first fundamental law of teaching thoroughly, and education will benefit immeasurably. This is the beginning of excellence.

The Law of the Learner

The Law

The learner must show interest in the material to be learned.

The learner must show interest
in the material
to be learned.

The Philosophy of the Law

Like the law of the teacher, the law of the learner is almost a truism. Yet it is as profound as it is seemingly simple. Plain proof of its truth lies in the readiness with which everyone will admit it, yet its real significance comes into view only with careful study.

Showing interest means directing one's mind to some object. Of course, more mature minds have longer attention spans. The two chief hindrances to interest and attention are apathy and distraction. The former may be due to a lack of taste for the subject under consideration, or to weariness or some other physical condition. Distraction—division of attention among several objects—is a foe of all learning. If the apathy or distraction comes from fatigue or illness, the wise teacher will not attempt to force a pupil to learn.

Rules for Teachers

1. Never begin an exercise until the attention of the class has been secured. Study for a moment the faces of the pupils to see if all are mentally, as well as bodily, present.

2. Pause whenever attention is interrupted or lost, and wait until it is completely regained.

3. Never wholly exhaust the attention of your pupils. Stop as soon as signs of fatigue appear.

4. Adapt the length of the class exercise to the ages of the pupils; the younger the pupils, the briefer the lesson.

5. Arouse attention, when necessary, by variety in your presentation. But be careful to avoid distractions, keeping the real lesson in view.

6. Kindle and maintain the highest possible interest in the subject. Interest and attention interact with each other.

*The learner must show interest
in the material
to be learned.*

7. Present those aspects of the lesson and illustrations that correspond to the ages and attainments of the pupils.

8. Appeal whenever possible to the interests of your pupils.

9. Find out the favorite stories, songs, and subjects of the pupils, and make good use of them.

10. Look for sources of distraction, such as unusual noises inside the classroom and out, and reduce them to a minimum.

11. Prepare thought-provoking questions beforehand. Be sure that they are not beyond the age and attainment of your pupils.

12. Make your presentation as attractive as possible, using illustrations and legitimate visual aids. Do not, however, make these devices so prominent that they become sources of distraction.

13. Be an example of close attention to and genuine interest in the lesson. True enthusiasm is contagious.

14. Make good use of eye contact and gestures. Pupils respond to an earnest gaze and natural gestures.

Violations and Mistakes

1. Teachers err when they begin before gaining the attention of their pupils, or continue after losing it. One might just as well begin before the pupils have entered the room, or continue after they have left.

2. It is a mistake to urge pupils to listen after their power of attention has been exhausted, and when fatigue has set in.

3. Some teachers make little or no effort to discover the interests and experiences of their pupils, or to create a real interest in the subject. Such teachers seek to compel attention. This awakens disgust instead of delight.

4. Some teachers kill the power of atten-

The learner must show interest
in the material
to be learned.

---

tion in their pupils by failing to utilize any fresh ideas or to make any new, interesting statements to stimulate interest in the subject. They drone on through their work, thinking of it as routine. Naturally the pupils soon assume the same attitude.

It is no wonder that, through these and other violations of the law of the learner, our education is often unattractive and success so limited! If adherence to this rule is so important in schools, where the attendance of children is compelled, and where the paid instructor teaches with full authority of the law—it is all the more necessary in Christian education where attendance and learning are voluntary. The teacher who wins the richest and best results observes this law faithfully. All teachers should master the art of gaining and keeping attention, and of exciting genuine interest. They then will rejoice at the results of their work.

3

The Law of the Language

The Law

The language used in teaching must be common to the teacher and learner. In other words, it must be understood by and have the same meaning for both.

The language used in teaching
must be common
to the teacher and learner.

The Philosophy of the Law

The vocabulary of the teacher may be many times larger than that of the pupil. So the teacher, to be understood, must be sure his or her words fall within the range of the pupil's vocabulary. Outside of these limits, the language of the teacher will have little meaning or perhaps be grossly misunderstood. The greater the number of unfamiliar words, the less effective will be the teaching.

Rules for Teachers

1. Study constantly and carefully the language of the pupils to learn what words they use and what meaning they assign to them.
2. Determine the pupils' knowledge of the subject. Learn both their ideas and ways of expressing them.
3. Express yourself as far as possible in

the language of your pupils, carefully correcting any incorrect interpretations they may read into your words.

4. Use the simplest and the smallest possible number of words that will express your meaning. Unnecessary words increase the possibilities for misunderstanding.

5. Use short sentences with simple construction. Long sentences are difficult to understand and are frequently confusing to students.

6. If the listeners obviously fail to understand you, repeat your thought in other words, if possible with greater simplicity.

7. Help pupils grasp the meaning of your words by using illustrations. Natural objects and pictures are especially helpful for young children. Take illustrations from the listeners' own experiences whenever possible.

8. When it is necessary to teach a new word, explain its meaning before giving the word. This can be done best by simple il-

The language used in teaching
must be common
to the teacher and learner.

lustrations closely related to the students' own experience.

9. Try to increase the number of the pupils' words, and at the same time clarify meaning. Enlargement of vocabulary means an increase of the pupils' knowledge and power.

10. As the acquisition of language is one of the important aims in the process of education, do not be content to have your students listen in silence, no matter how attentive they are. Encourage them to talk freely about the material at hand.

11. Proceed *slowly*. Each word should be learned thoroughly before others are added.

12. Review and test frequently to make sure pupils understand the meanings of the new words you have used.

Violations and Mistakes

1. When pupils look interested, the teacher may be deceived into thinking that

the language is thoroughly understood. While pupils may appear to understand, they may be catching only a mere glimpse of the meaning.

2. Children are often entertained by the manner of the teacher. They may seem attentive to words when they are really watching only the teacher's eyes, lips, or actions. They will sometimes profess to understand simply to please their instructor and gain praise.

3. Misuse of language is one of the common faults in teaching. Some teachers attempt to cover up their own ignorance or indolence with a cloud of verbiage.

4. Many teachers have little appreciation of the wonderful character and complexity of language. They do not understand that modern society could scarcely exist without words and speech.

5. Teachers occasionally ignore the fact that many of the topics studied in school lie

Law 3

*The language used in teaching
must be common
to the teacher and learner.*

outside the daily life and language of the children. Every subject has a language of its own which must be mastered if the student is to make any progress in it. The teacher in Christian education should recognize that here lies a problem. Many times the facts and truths of religion are likely to be distorted by the half-understood terms in which they are conveyed. Teaching Bible truths to children requires that we make our words clear.

6. Likewise, the preacher with a seminary degree and an understanding of Hebrew and Greek would do well to consider the vocabulary and experience of the persons in the pew. Common words with illustrations often communicate far better than do theological pronouncements. Consider that Jesus, the Master Teacher, effectively used parables to teach significant truths.

The Law of
the Lesson

The Law

The truth to be taught must be learned through truth already known. That is, the new and unknown can be explained only by the familiar and the known.

The truth to be taught
must be learned
through truth already known.

The fourth law is the core of teaching. This law is not as simple or obvious as the laws already given. But it is perhaps even more important. The first three laws dealt with the teacher, the learner, and the language which is the medium of communication between them. The fourth law deals with the lesson—the teacher's passing on to the pupils the experience and principles that will be active forces in their lives. And at the same time the teacher furnishes students with means of research and further study. All of this is the very heart of the work of the teacher.

The Philosophy of the Law

All teaching must begin at some point. If the subject is new, the teacher must find a point at which the subject bears some likeness to something known and familiar. Even with adults, skillful educators struggle to find some comparison with familiar experiences. Before proceeding they seek a parallel between what is unknown and something already known. Until this starting point is found, it is useless to go on. To do so is like telling someone to follow you over a winding path in the darkness without first letting the person know where you are starting on the path. Naturally, if adults must have such an aid, children can't be expected to learn without it. Often pupils explain their inability to understand the lesson by the simple statement: "I didn't know what the teacher was talking about!" The fault lies distinctly with the teacher, not the student.

From its starting point, all teaching advances in some direction. Properly, teaching should advance toward the acquisition of new experiences. It is a serious error to keep the studies of pupils too long on familiar

Law 4

*The truth to be taught
must be learned
through truth already known.*

ground on the assumption that this is necessary for thoroughness.

Learning should proceed by graded steps which link every fact or concept to another. Simple and concrete facts lead naturally to general and abstract ideas, as premises lead to conclusions, and as an understanding of natural phenomena leads to laws. Each new idea mastered becomes a part of the knowledge of the student, and serves as a starting point for a fresh advance.

Rules for Teachers

What we call knowledge is often a record of solved problems. Facts have been collected and tested and organized into laws and systems. They represent the results of facing situations and finding things out first hand. In passing knowledge on to others, the more closely we can approximate real, vital situations, the better will be our teaching. There are some who go so far as to say that no attempt should be made to impart knowledge unless the student feels a distinct need for it—unless it deals with a real-life situation. This is not always possible, but it is incumbent upon the teacher to know what the experiences of the student are and to keep them in mind so that the instruction may be as rich and meaningful as possible.

1. Find out what your pupils know of the subject you wish to teach them. This is your starting point. It includes textbook knowledge and all information that they may possess, however acquired.

2. Make the most of the pupils' knowledge and experience. Let them feel its importance as a means to further knowledge.

3. Encourage your pupils to clarify and freshen their knowledge by talking about it.

*The truth to be taught
must be learned
through truth already known.*

---

4. Begin with facts or ideas known by your pupils. Take steps from what is already familiar. Geography naturally begins with the hometown, history with the pupils' own memories, and morals with their own consciences.

5. Relate every lesson as much as possible to former lessons and the pupils' knowledge and experience.

6. Arrange your presentation so that each step of the lesson leads easily and naturally to the next.

7. Proportion the steps of the lesson to the ages and attainments of your pupils. Do not discourage children with lessons or exercises that are too long. On the other hand, do not fail to rise to the expectations of older pupils by giving them lessons that are too easy.

8. Find illustrations from real life and familiar objects related to the teaching content.

9. Lead students to find illustrations from their own experience.

10. Make every new fact or principle familiar to your pupils. Try to establish and entrench it firmly, so that it will be available for use in explaining new material to come.

11. Urge students to make use of their own knowledge and attainments in every way that is practicable. This will lead to new knowledge. Teach them that knowledge is power by showing how knowledge helps to solve problems.

12. Make every advance clear and familiar, so that the progress to the next step is on known ground.

13. As far as possible, choose the problems which you give to your students from their own experience. Use real and not artificial problems.

14. Remember that your pupils are learning to think, and that to think properly, they

The truth to be taught
must be learned
through truth already known.

___

must learn to face intelligently and reflec-
tively the problems posed by their school
work and life outside of school.

Violations and Mistakes

1. It is not unusual for teachers to introduce new lessons, or even new subjects, for
which pupils have not been prepared by
previous study or by their experience.

2. Before beginning a subject, many
teachers fail to ascertain exactly what their
students already know.

3. A common error is failure to connect
new lessons with those that have gone before. Some teachers treat each lesson as if
it were independent of all the others.

4. Oftentimes past learnings are consid-
ered goods stored away instead of instru-
ments for further use.

5. Too often elementary facts and definitions are not made thoroughly familiar.

6. Sometimes new steps are attempted before the previous ones are thoroughly understood.

7. Some teachers err in assigning lessons or exercises that are too long for the concentration of their students.

8. Teachers frequently fail to encourage students to think of themselves as discoverers. Children, especially, should be encouraged to discover new truths by using what they have already been taught.

9. A common fault is failure to show the connections between parts of the subject that have been taught and parts that are yet to come.

As a consequence of these and other violations of the law of the lesson, much teaching is poor, and its benefits, if any, are fleeting. The pupils acquire very little

*The truth to be taught
must be learned
through truth already known.*

knowledge and do not develop the power of studying for themselves. This is as true of Biblical knowledge as of any other. Instead of being viewed as a related whole, the Bible is occasionally viewed as scattered parts, like bits of broken glass. The effect many times is only to puzzle and confuse, rather than to clarify by relating the parts to the whole.

The Law of the Teaching Process

The Law

Teaching must excite and direct self-activity by the pupils. As a rule, teaching should tell them nothing that they can learn for themselves.

*Teaching must excite
and direct self-activity
by the pupils.*

The law of the teacher dealt essentially with one's qualifications. Here we deal with the teacher's function. The actual work of the teacher consists of awakening the mind of the pupil and setting in action student self-activities. Knowledge cannot simply be passed from mind to mind. Rather, knowledge must in every case be recognized and rethought and relived by the receiving mind. All explanation and exposition are useless except as they serve to excite and direct the student to thinking. If the pupil is not stimulated to think and act, teaching has no results. The words of the teacher are falling upon deaf ears.

The Philosophy of the Law

There are a few cases in which it may be expedient to disregard the law of the teaching process. For example, it may be disregarded in the interest of time or in the case of a very weak or discouraged pupil. Or when intense interest has been aroused and there is a keen demand for information that the teacher can give quickly and effectively. But as a general rule, make your pupils discoverers of truth—make them find out for themselves! This fundamental truth has been stated in various ways: Wake up your pupils' minds! Set the pupils to thinking! Arouse the spirit of inquiry! Get your pupils to work! All these familiar maxims are different expressions of this law.

Rules for Teachers

1. Adapt lessons and assignments to the ages and experiences of your students. Very young children will be interested in what appeals to the senses. The more mature will

---

Law 5

Teaching must excite
and direct self-activity
by the pupils.

be attracted by problems demanding reasoning and reflection.

2. Select lessons which relate to the environment and needs of the students.

3. Find a point where the subject and the lesson to be taught make contact with the lives of your students.

4. Excite interest in the lesson, as soon as it is assigned, by asking some question or making some statement relating it to the students' experience. Assure them that something worth knowing is to be found out if the lesson is thoroughly studied. Later, be sure to ask for the truths discovered.

5. Imagine that you too are a pupil, and join in the search for facts, principles, and skills.

6. Repress impatience for the students to explain what they are learning. They will resent it, and will feel that they could have answered had you given time.

7. In all class exercises aim to excite fresh

interest and activity. Suggest questions for the students to investigate out of class. The lesson that does not culminate in fresh questions is unsuccessful.

8. Observe each student to see that minds are not wandering from the lesson at hand.

9. Count it your chief duty to awaken the minds of your pupils, and do not rest until each student shows mental activity by asking questions.

10. Repress the desire to tell all you know or think about the lesson or subject. If you do say something by way of illustration or explanation, introduce a fresh question.

11. Give students time to think, after you are sure that minds are actively at work. Encourage them to ask questions when they are puzzled.

12. Do not answer too promptly the questions asked, but restate them to give them greater force and breadth. Often answer by asking new questions to stimulate deeper thought.

*Teaching must excite
and direct self-activity
by the pupils.*

_____

13. Teach pupils to ask What? Why? and How?—the nature, cause and method of every fact or principle taught them. Good questions also include Where? When? By whom? and What then?—the place, time, agents, and consequences of events.

14. Do not exhaust a subject, but leave additional work to stimulate the thought and the efforts of your students.

Violations and Mistakes

1. The chief violation of the law of the teaching process consists of attempts to force lessons by simply telling facts. "I have told you ten times, and yet you don't know!" exclaims a teacher who fails to realize that knowing comes by thinking, not by being told.

2. Another mistake is to blame the pupil's memory for not retaining what it never really held. If facts or principles are to be

remembered, the attention must be concentrated upon them for some time, and there must be a conscious effort to remember.

3. Teachers also err when they require pupils to repeat the very words of the book. If you ask a question in class, don't refuse pupils time to think. If a pupil hesitates for lack of a pertinent thought, or in apparent failure of memory, the fault lies in yesterday's teaching. Its deficiencies show fruit today. If a pupil hesitates out of slowness of thinking, or because of the difficulty of the subject, then time should be given for additional thought. If the period will not permit it, let the answer hold over until the next class.

A hurried and unreflective recital of the facts of the lesson lies at the base of the superficial and impractical character of much of today's teaching. Instead of learning thoroughly the material of our lessons, we endeavor to learn it only so as to recite the

*Teaching must excite
and direct self-activity
by the pupils.*

facts promptly. If faults of this character are detrimental in our public schools, how much more serious are they in Christian education! The lessons of Christian teachers must carry over into the lives of their pupils, making them wise in the religious truths taught them. So instruction must not be mere recital, but must employ stimulating teaching methods.

How different are the results when the law of the teaching process is properly followed! Students think for and direct themselves, and the classroom is transformed into a busy laboratory. The pupils become thinkers and discoverers. They master great truths, and apply them to the great questions of life. They invade new fields of knowledge. The teacher merely leads the march. Their reconnaissance becomes a conquest. Skill and power grow with the exercise of the mind. Through this process, the students find out what their minds are for, and become students of life.

The Law of the Learning Process

The Law

Pupils must reproduce in their own minds the truths to be learned.

Pupils must reproduce
in their own minds
the truths to be learned.

We have seen that the teacher's work consists essentially in arousing and guiding self-activities by the pupils. While the laws of the teaching and learning processes may seem at first to be only different aspects of the same law, they are really quite distinct—the one applying to the work of the instructor, the other to the work of those receiving instruction. The law of the teaching process involves the means by which self-activities are to be awakened; the law of the learning process determines the nature of these activities.

Observe children as they study, and note carefully what they do. It's not a vague and purposeless exertion of powers. There is a clear and distinct act of process. They form in their minds, by the use of their own powers, a concept of the facts, principles, or skills in the lesson. This is the purpose to which all the efforts of teacher and pupil must be directed.

The Philosophy of the Law

Merely pouring out the content of one's knowledge is not teaching. Likewise, true learning is not memorization and repetition of the words and ideas of the teacher. The work of education, contrary to the common understanding, is much more the work of the pupil than of the teacher. This idea is fundamental.

No real learning is wholly a repetition of the thoughts of others. The discoverer borrows facts known to others and then adds what he or she knows from personal experience. The aim should be to become an independent searcher in the fields of knowledge, not merely a passive learner from others. Both the original investigator and the student must be seekers for new facts and principles, and both must aim to gain clear conceptions of those facts and

*Pupils must reproduce
in their own minds
the truths to be learned.*

principles. It is indispensable that the student become an investigator.

Pupils are sometimes believed to have learned the lesson when they have committed it to memory, and can repeat or recite it word for word. This is all that is attempted by many pupils and required by some teachers. They consider their work done if they can secure verbatim reproductions. Education would be cheap and easy if this were real and valuable learning.

Rather than memorizing words, however, the pupil must have an understanding of what is taught. The teacher should stimulate the pupil to ask questions like, What does the lesson say? What is its meaning? How can I express this meaning in my own language? Do I believe what the lesson tells me, and why? What is the good of it—how may I apply and use the knowledge which it gives? No lesson is really learned until the pupil has answered these questions.

Variations in the Law

1. It should be remembered that the mental activity of young children lies close to the senses. Their understanding of a lesson will be largely confined to facts which appeal to the eye, or which can be illustrated to the senses. A little later the desire of pupils for carrying on some active enterprise may profitably be utilized in their training. As maturity is approached, young people think more and more about reasons, and the lessons which will appeal most to them will be the ones which emphasize reasons and which lead to conclusions.

2. The operation of the law of the learning process will vary to meet the conditions of the different fields of human knowledge. The capable teacher will discover how each separate field can be most successfully studied.

*Pupils must reproduce
in their own minds
the truths to be learned.*

Rules for Teachers

1. Help pupils to form a clear idea of the work to be done.

2. Inform them that the words of the lesson have been carefully chosen, that they may have special meanings which it may be important to find out.

3. Emphasize that usually more things are implied than are said.

4. Ask the pupils to express, in their own words, the meaning of the lesson as they understand it, and to persist until they have the whole idea.

5. Aim to make the pupils independent investigators, that is, students of nature and seekers after truth. Cultivate the habit of research and action as a result of the lesson.

6. Constantly seek to develop in pupils a profound regard for truth as something noble, worthwhile, and enduring.

Violations and Mistakes

1. Pupils are sometimes left in the twilight of an imperfect and fragmentary mastery by a failure to think the lesson into clearness. The teacher's haste to go on often precludes time for thinking.

2. Occasionally the language of the textbook is so insisted upon that pupils have no incentive to try their own power of expression. Thus they are taught to feel that the words are everything and the meaning nothing. For example, students often learn the demonstrations of geometry by heart, and do not suspect that there is any meaning in them.

3. Failure to insist upon original thinking by the pupils is one of the most common faults of our schools.

4. Frequently no reason is asked for the statements in the lesson, and none is given.

*Pupils must reproduce
in their own minds
the truths to be learned.*

The pupil believes what the book says, simply because the book says it.

5. Practical applications are persistently neglected. That the lesson has a use is the last thought to enter the minds of many pupils.

Violations of the law of the learning process are perhaps the most common and most fatal of any in education. Since the work of learning is the very heart of education, a failure here is a failure in all. Knowledge may be placed before the pupils in endless profusion and in the most attractive way. Teachers may pour out instruction without let-up. Lessons may be recited under the pressure of the most effective discipline and of the most urgent appeals. But if this law is not followed, learning will fall short of its mark!

Nowhere are these faults in teaching more frequent or more serious than in the Sunday school. "Always learning, but never able to come to a knowledge of the truth," is the sad story of many Sunday-school classes. If these classes were taught as this law prescribes, the results in the lives of the students would be very different.

The Law of Review and Application

The Law

Teaching must be completed, confirmed, and tested by review and application.

Teaching must be completed,
confirmed, and tested
by review and application.

Let us now suppose the process of teaching to be completed. The teacher and the pupils have met and have done their work together. Language freighted with ideas and aided with illustrations has been spoken and understood. Knowledge has been placed in the minds of the pupils, and it lies there, more or less complete to feed thought, to guide and modify actions and to form character. The teacher's work seems ended. Yet perhaps the most difficult task remains.

All that has been accomplished is hidden in the minds of the pupils, and there it lies as a potential rather than as a possession. What process can fix into active habits the thoughts which have been taught? What influence can mold into permanent ideals the conceptions that have been gained? This final and finishing work is the concern of the seventh and last law.

There are three chief aims of review: (1) to perfect knowledge, (2) to confirm knowledge, and (3) to render knowledge ready and useful. These three aims, though different, are achieved by the same process. It would be difficult to overstate the value and importance of review. No time in teaching is spent more profitably than that spent in reviewing. Other things being equal, the ablest and most successful teacher is the one who reviews frequently, thoroughly, and interestingly.

The Philosophy of the Law

A review is more than repetition. A machine may repeat a process, but only an intelligent agent can review it. Repetition done by a machine is a second action precisely like the first. Review by the mind is the rethinking of a thought. It involves fresh conceptions and new associations, and increases the usefulness of knowledge.

Teaching must be completed,
confirmed, and tested
by review and application.

A partial review may embrace a single lesson, or it may include a single topic of the subject. It may develop a single fact or principle, or recall an event or a difficult point or question. A complete review may be a cursory reviewing of the whole field through a few general questions, or it may be a full and final reconsideration of all teaching covered. Each kind of review has its place and use. No teaching can be complete without a review made either under the teacher's direction or voluntarily by the pupil.

A new lesson or a fresh topic never reveals all of itself at first. It attracts attention and its novelties may dazzle the mind. When we enter a strange house, we do not know the exact location of its several rooms, and our attention is drawn to a few of the more singular and conspicuous pieces of furniture or decorations. We must return again and again, and resurvey the scene with eyes grown familiar to the place, before we can grasp the whole plan of the building and become familiar with the various rooms and furniture. So also we must return again and again to a lesson if we are to see all there is in it, and come to a full understanding.

Practical assignments should not be neglected. The mind and hand are capable teachers, and few reviews are more effective than those which utilize a hands-on approach. Consider the power and value of laboratory work, so common in all scientific, artistic, and vocational study. Lists of persons, objects, and places mentioned in the lessons; summaries of facts or events; maps, plans, and drawings are also of valuable assistance in reviewing. Tests, if properly designed to use students' mental abilities rather than to force regurgitation of memorized material, can be helpful in reviews.

Teaching must be completed,
confirmed, and tested
by review and application.

Rules for Teachers

1. Consider reviews as always appropriate.

2. Have set times for review. At the beginning of each period, review briefly the preceding lesson. But vary the technique.

3. At the close of each lesson, glance back at the ground which has been covered. Almost every good lesson closes with a summary. Sometimes pupils may be called upon to summarize the lesson at the close of the class period.

4. After five or six lessons, or at the close of a topic, review the material from the beginning.

5. Whenever a reference to former lessons can profitably be made, do so. This will bring old knowledge into fresh light.

6. Make sure new lessons review and apply the material of former lessons.

7. Make the first review as soon as practicable after a lesson is learned.

8. In order to make reviews easily and rapidly, keep in mind the material that has been learned. If it is ready for instant use, you will be able to begin at any time an impromptu review in any part of the field. The pupils, seeing that their teacher thinks it worthwhile to remember and recall what has been studied, will desire to do the same, and will work to make themselves ready for review questions.

9. Come up with new questions on old lessons, new illustrations for old texts, new proof for old statements, new applications of old truths. This will give the pupil fresh interest in old material, thus affording a profitable review.

10. Never omit a final review. It should be searching, comprehensive, and masterful, bringing together the different topics which have been studied.

11. *Find as many applications as possible.*

*Teaching must be completed,
confirmed, and tested
by review and application.*

Every thoughtful application involves a useful and effective review.

12. Do not forget the value of exercises which involve hands-on activities as well as the mind. Use them frequently in review. Pupils will soon learn to come to their classes ready to ask and answer questions.

Violations and Mistakes

Lack of proper review is not the sole cause of failure in teaching. However, a wider and more thorough use of the principle of review would go far to improve teaching. We don't pour water into broken pots. While good reviews might not increase the quality of educational water which goes in, they would help stop the leaks. Consider the following teaching errors:

1. The ineffective teacher often totally neglects review.

2. Hurried and impatient teachers give a

wholly inadequate review. They are often more concerned with getting through the work of the term or semester than making the work the pupils' own.

3. Another mistake is that of delaying all review work until the end of the semester or term. The material of the course is by then largely forgotten, and the review amounts to little more than a poor relearning, with little interest and less value.

4. Other teachers make review a process of lifeless and colorless repetition of questions and answers. Often the very questions and answers which were originally used are used again. This is a review in name only.

The law of review, given full force, requires that there be fresh vision, that is, a clear rethinking and reusing of the material which has been learned. Review is like the finishing touches of the artist to a masterful painting.

Conclusion

Let us summarize once again the seven laws of teaching:

1. The excellent teacher must be equipped with the knowledge he or she wishes to communicate.

2. The pupils must fix their attention and interest on the subject or material to be learned.

3. The language used in teaching must be clear, simple, and easily understood by both teacher and pupil.

4. The lesson, the knowledge, or experience to be transmitted must be communicated in terms of truths already known by the learners.

5. The teacher must arouse and direct self-activities by the pupils, thus stimulating them to learn for themselves.

6. The pupils must reproduce in their own thought, step by step—first in mere outline and then in full and finished conception—the lesson to be learned.

7. The material studied should be tested, corrected, completed, confirmed, and applied through a systematic process of review.

These are the great natural laws governing the complex process by which a human intelligence gains knowledge, attitudes, and skill. While study of these laws may not make every reader an excellent teacher, they will, when fully observed, produce their effects with the same certainty that scientific, natural, and spiritual laws produce their effects.